¡Vamos a Escuchar! 2

A Listening Comprehension Course for Leaving Certificate Spanish

Rosemary Graham B.A., M. Litt.

FOLENS

Acknowledgements

The author wishes to thank the following: Folens editor Priscilla O'Connor, and John O'Connor of Folens Publishers, for their support, my friend Yolanda Quintanilla Aparicio for her invaluable assistance when clarification was sought, recording artists Sonia de Acuña Roldán, Montserrat Calvo Velo, Cristina Centallas Alarcón, Antonio Echvarria Suárez, Iñaki Hernández Lasa, David Martínez Carballo, Francisco Merino Alonso, José Luis Oliver Egea, Marian Ordóñez, Jaime Ortega Montero, Montserrat de Pablo, Cristina Rodríguez Guntín, Paulo Rodriguez Fernández, Begoña Serrano, Yolanda Quintanilla Aparicio and Amor Valero, artist Aileen Caffrey for the delightful illustrations, Paul Waldron of All Write Media and sound engineer Gar Duffy for his expertise and immense patience. Finally, I would like to thank my husband Bernard and our children for their encouragement and support during the preparation of this course.

Editor: Priscilla O'Connor

Design: Karen Hoey

Layout: Oisín Burke

Illustrations: Aileen Caffrey, Gary Dermody

© Rosemary Graham 2009

Produced in Ireland by Folens Publishers, Hibernian Industrial Estate, Greenhills Road, Tallaght, Dublin 24

ISBN: 978-1-84741-242-3

The author and publisher wish to acknowledge the following for permission to reproduce photographs: Alamy Images, Getty Images.

All rights reserved. No part of this publication may be reproduced or transmitted in any form or by any means (stencilling, photocopying, etc.) for whatever purpose, even purely educational, without written permission from the publisher.

The publisher reserves the right to change, without further notice at any time, the specification of this product, whether by change of materials, colours, bindings, format, text revision or any other characteristic.

Contents

Foreword		vii
Unit 1	¿Me ayuda, por favor?	1
Unit 2	¡Lo que sufrimos las madres!	2
Unit 3	Mensajes telefónicos (1)	3
Unit 4	¡Problemas!	4
Unit 5	Una compañía de investigación de márketing llama a la Sra. Martín	5
Unit 6	¿Un trabajo así? ¡Ni en sueños!	6
Unit 7	Una encuesta sobre los bolsos	7
Unit 8	Comprando	8
Unit 9	Un camarero distraído	9
Unit 10	Un día típico de escuela	10
Unit 11	¿Le ayudo en algo?	12
Unit 12	Noticias (1)	13
Unit 13	¡Manos a la obra!	14
Unit 14	Anuncios (1)	15
Unit 15	Mis ilusiones para el futuro	16
Unit 16	Mensajes telefónicos (2)	17
Unit 17	Susana organiza una fiesta sorpresa	18
Unit 18	Una reclamación	19
Unit 19	Noticias (2)	20
Unit 20	En una Escuela de Idiomas de Dublín	22
Unit 21	Tortilla de patatas	23
Unit 22	Zapatos extraviados	24
Unit 23	Anuncios (2)	25
Unit 24	El Zoo Safari	27
Unit 25	El tiempo (1)	29
Unit 26	Un minuto de tu tiempo	30
Unit 27	Mensajes telefónicos (3)	31

Unit 28	Una visita relámpago a Valencia	32
Unit 29	¡Vaya fiasco de viaje!	33
Unit 30	Rosa hace una entrevista	34
Unit 31	¿Por qué te llamas así?	36
Unit 32	Martín pide un favor a su madre	37
Unit 33	Anuncios (3)	38
Unit 34	En la oficina de turismo	39
Unit 35	Un perro muy leal	40
Unit 36	Planes para el sábado	41
Unit 37	Philip Treacy: sombrerero extraordinario	42
Unit 38	En la oficina de objetos perdidos	43
Unit 39	Dos sucesos desagradables	44
Unit 40	Noticias (3)	45
Unit 41	Champiñones rellenos	46
Unit 42	La casa donde vivo	47
Unit 43	El tiempo (2)	49
Unit 44	Cosas que me fastidian	51
Unit 45	Mensajes de texto	52
Unit 46	Cuando era niña	53
Unit 47	Una excursión de fin de curso	55
Unit 48	Planes para el verano	57
Unit 49	Regalos de Navidad	58
Unit 50	En un restaurante	60
Unit 51	Vuelta a España	62
Unit 52	Accidentes de tráfico	63
Unit 53	En el mercado	64
Unit 54	Facebook	65
Unit 55	Noticias (4)	66
Unit 56	El botellón	68
Unit 57	En el cámping	70
Unit 58	Una riña	72

Unit 59	La dieta española	73
Unit 60	En el piso de al lado	74
Unit 61	Noticias (5)	76
Unit 62	Un cliente poco contento	77
Unit 63	Medina Azahara	79
Unit 64	Maite toma parte en un concurso de radio	80
Unit 65	¿De verdad? ¡Sí!	82
Unit 66	El Sr. Lázaro va de compras	84
Unit 67	El día que más recuerdo	85
Unit 68	El Tibidabo	87
Unit 69	Una pequeña visita a Francia	88
Unit 70	El tiempo (3)	90
Unit 71	El sitio que más me gusta	91
Unit 72	Exámenes	92
Unit 73	Noticias (6)	94
Unit 74	¿Cómo pasas las Navidades?	96
Unit 75	Anuncios (4)	98
Unit 76	Un día catastrófico	99
Unit 77	Unas costumbres españolas	100
Unit 78	El tiempo (4)	102
Unit 79	La persona que más admiro	104
Unit 80	Algunas fiestas locales de España	106
Unit 81	Unas gemelas extraordinarias	108
Unit 82	En la consulta	110
Unit 83	Noticias (7)	112
Unit 84	¡Que aproveche!	114
Unit 85	¿La correspondencia más breve del mundo?	116
Unit 86	Natalia se encuentra depre	117
Unit 87	Pepe y Concha hacen una lluvia de ideas sobre el medio ambiente	119

Unit 88	Adolfo: ex drogadicto	121
Unit 89	Mousse de verano	123
Unit 90	La mujer en la España actual	124
Unit 91	El 11-M	127
Unit 92	Problemas actuales en España	129
Unit 93	Las cuevas de Altamira	131

Foreword

This second edition of *¡Vamos a Escuchar!* 2 features much new and revised material.

- The course has been extended to include several new units, a number of which have been designed to cater for transition-year students and weaker senior-cycle groups.
- Many other units have been revised and updated.
- New idioms and other vocabulary have been included to reflect current usage.
- The information provided in the units has been carefully researched to ensure that it is accurate and up to date, e.g. statistics, dates and cultural references.
- The course reflects the widespread use of modern communications technologies such as the mobile phone, iPods and the Internet.
- Students are encouraged to develop an interest in Spanish culture through references to festivals, customs and traditions, places of interest, social history, recent cultural changes, television programmes, food and drink and other areas of contemporary interest.
- A total of 16 native Spanish speakers from various areas took part in the recordings. Students have therefore the benefit of exposure to a wide variety of regional accents.
- All units and subunits are separately tracked on the CDs for ease of use, and the corresponding track numbers clearly referenced in the student's and teacher's book.

The main aim of language acquisition is communication and the listening skill is a fundamental part of this interaction. *¡Vamos a Escuchar!* 2 is a listening comprehension course which follows on the course material presented in *¡Vamos a Escuchar!* 1. It is designed to provide extensive practice in aural skills from lower intermediate to upper intermediate level. The course consists of two CDs of approximately two and a half hours' duration containing 93 units of recorded material, a student's book of comprehension questions based on the recordings and a teacher's transcript of the texts. It is suitable for both classroom and independent use.

The level of the units is graduated, leading to that typically used in the Leaving Certificate aural examination and a little beyond, so as to challenge the top students. However, every effort has been made to encourage all users to progress successfully through the course. The units cover a wide range of text types reflecting those commonly used in the Leaving Certificate aural examination, and include dialogues, telephone messages, telephone conversations, news items, weather forecasts, announcements, advertisements, narratives, interviews, recipes and monologues. Students are thus exposed to a wide range of language situations and registers typically encountered in a Spanish-speaking environment. Special emphasis is given to text types often causing particular difficulty, such as news items.

The units are carefully graded to present and reinforce key lexical and grammatical aspects of language appropriate to this level. Particular attention is given to areas commonly requiring reinforcement such as verb tense and form, the subjunctive mood, impersonal verbs, the imperative, adjective agreement, pronouns and numbers. The comprehension questions include a variety of formats such as straight questions, multiple-choice questions and true/false statements.

The Leaving Certificate examination places heavy emphasis on the aural skill, an indication of its importance in language acquisition. ¡Vamos a Escuchar! 2 provides an opportunity for extensive practice in this area. On completing this course students should not only be well prepared for any aural examination of upper intermediate level but more importantly be capable of surviving in a Spanish-speaking environment.

A Note on CD Track Numbering

Two CDs are supplied with this book. CD 1 covers Units 1–48 and CD 2 covers Units 49–93. Each unit or subunit has a corresponding CD track number, which is represented by a colour-coded icon, maroon for CD 1 and green for CD 2.

For example: means CD 1, track 2;

 means CD 2, track 12.

To David, Cathy, Michael, Kevin and Brendan

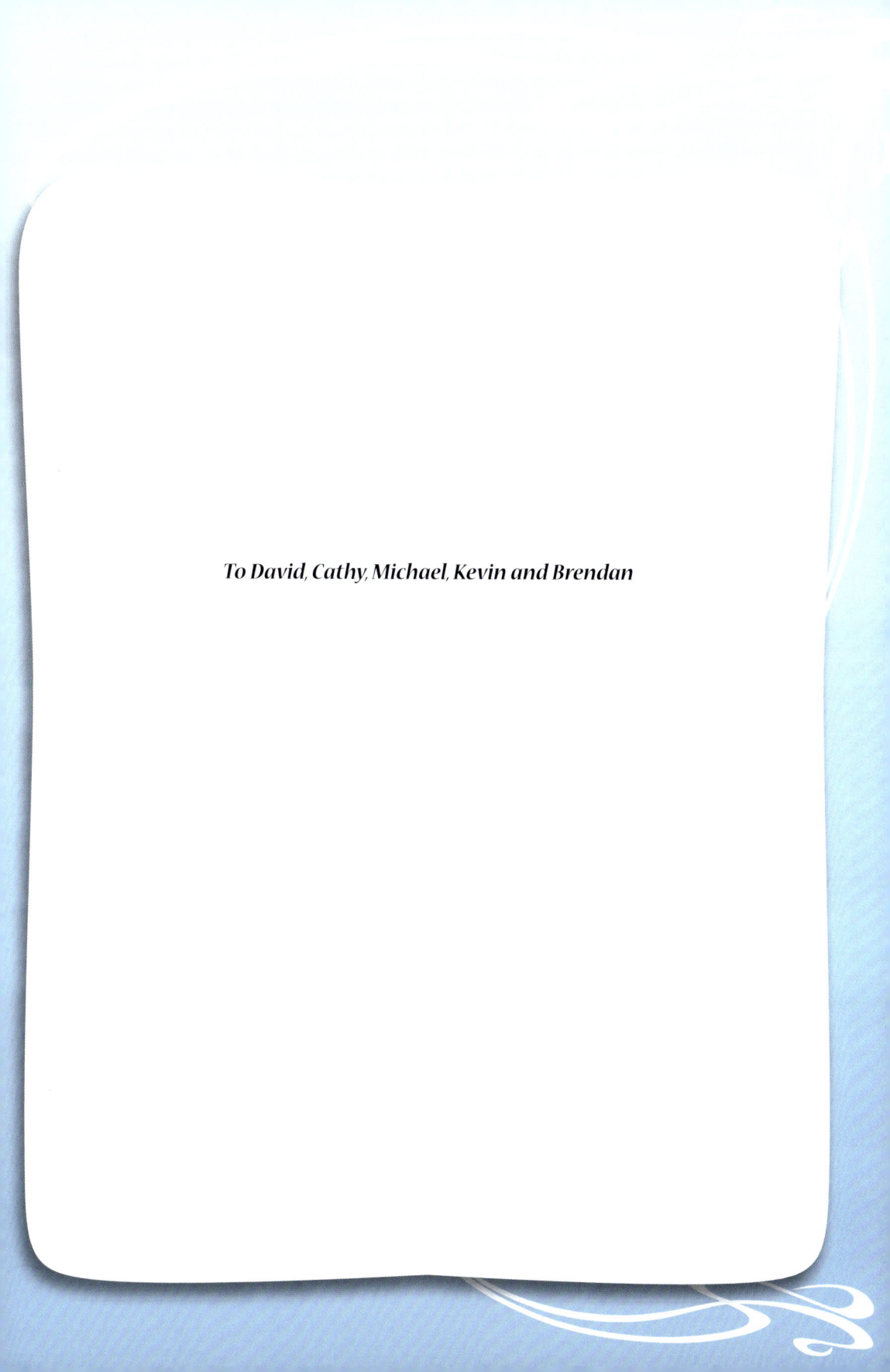

¡Vamos a escuchar 2!

1. ¿Me ayuda, por favor?

Some visitors to the town ask for help.

🔘 2–4

1. At which bus-stop does this young woman wish to get off the bus?
   ....

2. What does she ask the man beside her to do?
   ....

* * *

3. How much will this woman be fined if she parks in the street? ....

4. Where exactly does the man suggest she could park?
   ....

* * *

5. This young man is looking for:

   (a) a bar.   (b) a shop.   (c) a youth hostel.

   Put the correct letter in the box. ☐

6. How many minutes by foot will it take him to reach his destination? ....

¡Vamos a escuchar 2!

2. ¡Lo que sufrimos las madres!

Juan's mother is in a bad mood.

🔴 5

1. What did Juan's mother find on the table of his bedroom?
   ....
2. What did he leave on his bed? ....
3. Why is he reluctant to tidy his room just now?
   ....
4. Why does he have to use the computer a lot at the moment?
   ....
5. What does his mother reckon he spends a lot of money on?
   ....
6. Who is Montse? ....
7. According to Juan, what do some youths in his area spend their money on?
   ....
8. What does his mother say she will do? ....

¡Vamos a escuchar 2!

3. Mensajes telefónicos (1)

You will hear three telephone messages.

🔘 6-8

1. At what time does Marta phone her mother? ....
2. What are she and Clara doing? ....
3. What two suggestions has Clara's mother made to Marta?
   ....

* * *

4. How is a toothache affecting this person? ....
5. What has he been doing for the last two days?
   ....
6. When is he hoping to get a dental appointment? ....
7. What is his telephone number? ....

* * *

8. From what city is Laura phoning? ....
9. What age is her father? ....
10. What kind of voucher has she bought him? ....
11. For how long is the voucher valid? ....
12. When will she try to phone again? ....

¡Vamos a escuchar 2!

4. ¡Problemas!

Some people have a problem.

🔘 9–11

1. Why does a policeman stop this driver?

   ....

2. What excuse does the driver give him? ....

3. What does the policeman say will be the consequences of her action?

   (i) .... and (ii) ....

   ✳ ✳ ✳

4. What is the number of the flight this young woman was on? ....
5. When did the flight arrive? ....
6. What time is it now? ....
7. Describe her suitcase. ....
8. What phone number does the official tell her to contact? ....

   ✳ ✳ ✳

9. Describe the vase Manolito broke by accident. ....
10. Who bought the vase for his mother? ....
11. Why does his mother tell him not to worry? ....
12. What does she hope will not happen?

    ....

¡Vamos a escuchar 2!

5. Una compañía de investigación de márketing llama a la Sra. Martín

La Sra. Martín receives a phone call from a market research company.

🔘 12

1. How long does the caller say the phone call will take? ....
2. Give details of la Sra. Martín's family.
   ....
3. What do they normally have for breakfast?
   ....
4. What flavours of juice does she usually buy?
   ....
5. How many bottles of juice is the company going to send her? ....
6. What is her address?
   ....
7. On what date and at what time is the caller going to phone back?
   ....

¡Vamos a escuchar 2!

6. ¿Un trabajo así? ¡Ni en sueños!

Four young people say what job they would not like to have.

🔴 13–16

Speaker 1 would not like to be a .... because
  (i) ....
  (ii) ....
  (iii) ....

* * *

Speaker 2 would not like to be a .... because
  (i) ....
  (ii) ....
  (iii) ....

* * *

Speaker 3 would not like to be a .... because
  (i) ....
  (ii) ....
  (iii) ....

* * *

Speaker 4 would not like to be a .... because
  (i) ....
  (ii) ....
  (iii) ....

¡Vamos a escuchar 2!

7. Una encuesta sobre los bolsos

You will hear some information regarding a real survey which was carried out in Spain to find out about the handbags that Spanish women use.

🔘 17

1. How many women took part in this survey? ....
2. Between what ages were the women who took part? ....
3. According to the survey, what size of handbag do Spanish women prefer?
   ....
4. Most Spanish women prefer a handbag made of leather.   True ☐   False ☐
5. What is the average number of handbags which women from Cataluña own?
   ....
6. According to the survey, up to how many handbags do women from Madrid own? ....
7. Give details of the items that Spanish women typically carry in their handbag.
   ....
   ....
   ....
   ....

¡Vamos a escuchar 2!

8. Comprando

Four people are buying something.

🔘 18–21

1. Give details of the ice-cream that this woman is buying.
   ....
2. What else does she ask for? ....

* * *

3. What kind of ticket is this man buying? ....
4. What information does he ask for regarding the ticket?
   ....

* * *

5. What is the first item that this woman buys in the chemist's? ....
6. What is the second item that she wishes to buy, and why?
   ....

* * *

7. At what time is this film starting? ....
8. Where would this young man like to sit? ....
9. What else does the young man ask?
   ....

8

¡Vamos a escuchar 2!

9. Un camarero distraído

A waiter is somewhat absent-minded today!

🔊 22

1. Specify (a) the first course and (b) the second course that this woman ordered.
   (a) .... (b) ....
2. What did the waiter bring her by mistake? ....
3. What did she order to drink? ....
4. What drink did the waiter bring her instead? ....
5. What items are missing from the table? ....
6. Where has his wife gone? ....
7. Why is the waiter so distracted?
   ....
8. When is the waiter finishing work? ....
9. How long will the taxi take to bring him to his destination? ....

¡Vamos a escuchar 2!

10. Un día típico de escuela

Eva describes a typical school day.

🔘 23

1. At what time does Eva get up? ....
2. What does her school lunch consist of? ....
   ....
3. How does she get to school? ....
4. At what time do her classes begin? ....
5. What day does Eva give as an example? ....
6. What three subjects are studied before the break?
   (i) .... (ii) ....
   (iii) ....
7. The break is from .... to ....
8. What two subjects are taught between the break and lunch?
   (i) .... (ii) ....

¡Vamos a escuchar 2!

9. The lunch break is from .... to ....
10. In the afternoon Eva does: (a) yoga (b) aerobics. (c) home economics. (d) art.
    Put the correct letter in the box. ☐
11. What is her favourite subject? ....
12. Why does she find it easy? ....
13. Why does she dislike French? ....
14. At what time do classes finish? ....
15. What three things does Eva do at home before going to bed?
    (i) .... (ii) ....
    (iii) ....

¡Vamos a escuchar 2!

11. ¿Le ayudo en algo?

Three people are being attended to.

🔘 24–26

1. Describe the jacket that this woman has just seen in the shop-window.
   ....
2. What price is the jacket? ....
3. What size is she looking for? ....

* * *

4. What does this man wish to purchase? ....
5. What options does the shopkeeper give him? ....
6. What does he ask the shopkeeper regarding the item which he buys?
   ....
7. What does the shopkeeper tell him in reply? ....

* * *

8. For what dates does this woman wish to book a hotel room? ....
9. What kind of room does she require, and why?
   ....
10. What is the woman's surname? ....

¡Vamos a escuchar 2!

12. Noticias (1)

You will hear three news items.

🔊 27-29

1. When was this Picasso painting stolen? ....
2. In which city is the art gallery from which it was stolen? ....
3. How much is the painting worth? ....
4. What nationality is the suspected thief? ....
5. How did the police identify the suspected thief? ....

* * *

6. What (i) nationality and (ii) age is this Grand Prix rally driver?
   (i) .... (ii) ....
7. At what speed was he travelling when he crashed? ....
8. Describe his injuries. ....
   ....

* * *

9. Between what dates will the Cibeles fashion show take place? ....
10. How many (i) designers and (ii) fashion shows will there be?
    (i) .... (ii) ....
11. What colours will be in season this autumn? ....

¡Vamos a escuchar 2!

13. ¡Manos a la obra!

Alberto and his sister prepare dinner.

🔊 30

1. Why do Alberto and his sister have to prepare dinner?
   ....

2. Tick the ingredients that Alberto's sister mentions.

rice	☐	rabbit	☐
chicken	☐	stock cubes	☐
shellfish	☐	peas	☐
garlic	☐	onion	☐
salt	☐	pepper	☐
saffron	☐	colouring	☐

3. When did their mother go to the supermarket? ....
4. How long will the dinner take to prepare? ....
5. Why is Alberto anxious to finish quickly?
   ....

¡Vamos a escuchar 2!

14. Anuncios (1)

You will hear three advertisements.

🔊 31–33

1. How far is Port Aventura from (a) Barcelona and (b) the airport?
   (a) .... (b) ....
2. Besides a water-park and theme park, what other amenities are mentioned?
   ....
3. How many people have visited Port Aventura to date? ....
4. What is the telephone number of Port Aventura? ....
5. What is its website address? ....

* * *

6. What electrical items are reduced in this shop?
   ....
7. What other items are reduced? ....
8. On what day and at what time will the sale start? ....
9. What will the first ten lucky shoppers receive? ....

* * *

10. How many years' experience has the Armada School of English? ....
11. What is their telephone number? ....
12. What is their email address? ....
13. Give details of their office opening hours. ....

¡Vamos a escuchar 2!

15. Mis ilusiones para el futuro

Three young people talk about their hopes for the future.

🔵 34–36

1. What kind of person would this girl like to marry?
   ....

2. Why does she want to have a lot of children?
   ....

* * *

3. What profession does this speaker hope to have? ....

4. What country would she like to visit? ....

5. When did she make this decision?
   ....

* * *

6. What is this speaker's main ambition? ....

7. He proposes three ways of achieving it. What are they?

   (i) .... (ii) ....

   (iii) ....

8. Why does the third possibility not appeal to him? ....

¡Vamos a escuchar 2!

16. Mensajes telefónicos (2)

You will hear three telephone messages.

🔘 37–39

1. What is the number of the bus in which Teo is travelling? ....
2. When will he arrive at the terminal? ....
3. Why does he ask his father to pick him up?
   ....

* * *

4. From what country has Merche just returned? ....
5. On what day and at approximately what time is Merche hoping to meet up with her friends?
   ....
6. What does she ask Luci to do? ....

* * *

7. At what time does this man have to see his boss? ....
8. Why does this not suit him?
   ....
9. What does he say jokingly may be the reason his boss wants to see him?
   ....

17

¡Vamos a escuchar 2!

17. Susana organiza una fiesta sorpresa

Susana and her friend Marta plan a surprise birthday party for Susana's sister.

🔊 40

1. When is the birthday of Susana's sister? ....
2. What age will she be? ....
3. Why is Susana's sister not planning to celebrate her birthday?
   ....
4. Where are their parents at the moment? ....
5. How is Susana going to contact friends?

    (a) by phone   (b) by email   (c) by text message

    Put the correct letter in the box. ☐
6. Besides cold meats, what food does Susana suggest for the party?
   ....
7. What drinks does she suggest? ....
8. What does Susana nearly forget? ....
9. Why does Marta reckon they will have enough food and drink for the party?
   ....

¡Vamos a escuchar 2!

18. Una reclamación

Lola goes to a boutique to make a complaint.

🔴 41

1. When did Lola buy the jeans? ....
2. What two things are wrong with them?

   (i) .... (ii) ....
3. What size of jeans did Lola buy? ....
4. What does the shop assistant suggest happened?

   ....

5. The shop assistant says:

   (a) she will send them back to the factory.

   (b) she will speak to the manager of the shop.

   (c) Lola can have her money back.

   (d) Lola can choose something else.

   Put the correct letter in the box. ☐

¡Vamos a escuchar 2!

19. Noticias (2)

You will hear three news items.

🔊 42–44

1. How many people died in these traffic accidents? ....
2. When did the accidents occur? ....
3. How many people were (a) seriously injured and (b) slightly injured?
   (a) .... (b) ....
4. What two factors caused the pile-up in which 17 people died?
   (i) .... (ii) ....

* * *

5. What is the nationality of this missing girl? ....
6. What age is she? ....
7. Why was she in Motril? ....
8. Where did the search concentrate yesterday? ....
9. What does she look like? ....
10. What was she wearing when she disappeared?
    ....

* * *

¡Vamos a escuchar 2!

11. What is José Fernández's profession? ....
12. What is Loli's profession? ....
13. Why are they in the news? ....
14. What age is José? ....
15. What age is Loli? ....
16. Where and when did they meet? ....
17. What were they doing at the time? ....

¡Vamos a escuchar 2!

20. En una Escuela de Idiomas de Dublín

Pilar and Jesús meet during a coffee break at a Dublin School of English.

🔴 45

1. Besides food, what does Pilar miss about Spain? ....
2. What food does she miss? ....
   ....
3. She dislikes the cafés in Ireland.   True ☐   False ☐
4. How long does it take Jesús to get to Dublin city centre by bus? ....
5. When does he say the journey takes longer?
   ....
6. How long does he reckon the same journey would take by metro? ....
7. What things does Pilar find expensive in Ireland?
   ....
8. What does she suggest that she and Jesús will miss when they go back to Spain?
   ....

¡Vamos a escuchar 2!

21. Tortilla de patatas

You will hear a recipe for one of the most popular dishes in Spain: Spanish omelette.

🔘 46

1. How many eggs does this recipe require? ....
2. The potatoes are fried on a medium heat.   True ☐   False ☐
3. For how many minutes should the potatoes be fried? ....
4. For how long should the potatoes and beaten eggs be left resting? ....
5. What ingredient is fried while the potatoes and eggs are resting? ....
6. For approximately how many minutes should the first side of the omelette be cooked? ....
7. What suggestion is made when turning the omelette to the other side?
   ....
8. The omelette can be served hot or cold.   True ☐   False ☐

¡Vamos a escuchar 2!

22. Zapatos extraviados

Jorge mislays a pair of shoes.

🔵 47

1. Between what dates was Jorge staying in this Granada hotel?
   ....
2. What was the number of his bedroom? ....
3. Describe his shoes. ....
4. Where had he left them? ....
5. What reason does he give for forgetting his shoes?
   ....
6. What does the receptionist say she will do?
   ....

¡Vamos a escuchar 2!

23. Anuncios (2)

You will hear three advertisements.

🔘 48–50

1. Where is this restaurant situated? ....
2. What is said about the restaurant chefs? ....
3. Between what dates is there a special offer? ....
4. What exactly is the special offer?
   ....
5. What is the telephone number of the restaurant? ....

* * *

6. Between what dates is this Mediterranean cruise? ....
7. What cities will the ship visit?
   ....
8. The cruise offers full board.   True ☐   False ☐
9. What facilities does the cruise offer? ....
   ....

¡Vamos a escuchar 2!

10. What telephone number should people call for more details? ....

* * *

11. Why is this agency looking for models?

....

12. Over what age must models be? ....

13. What telephone number should they contact? ....

14. What details must they provide? ....

15. What is the email address of the model agency? ....

¡Vamos a escuchar 2!

24. El Zoo Safari

Adolfo telephones the Safari zoo to make some enquiries.

🔴 51

1. The opening times of the zoo are:

   Monday to Friday   from .... to ....

   Saturday and Sunday   from .... to ....

2. How long would one would need, in order to see the exhibits in the zoo?

   ....

3. Approximately how many species are there in the zoo? ....

4. Give full details of the ticket prices of the zoo. ....

   ....

5. What facilities does the zoo offer?

   ....

¡Vamos a escuchar 2!

6. What information is given regarding the birds of prey and sea lions?

　...

7. What is happening this Saturday, and why?

　...

8. What is Adolfo's Visa card number? ....

9. In what month does his Visa card expire? ....

10. Where can Adolfo collect the tickets that he buys? ....

¡Vamos a escuchar 2!

25. El tiempo (1)

You will hear a weather forecast.

🔵 52

1. It will be foggy in the Pyrenees.   True ☐   False ☐
2. In general it will be very sunny.   True ☐   False ☐
3. What will the maximum and minimum temperatures during the day be?

   maximum ………………………………   minimum ………………………………………

4. In which part of the country will night-time temperatures be lowest?

   ……………………………………………………………………………………………………

¡Vamos a escuchar 2!

26. Un minuto de tu tiempo

A radio host interviews Natuca, an international singer.

🔵 53

1. On what date is Natuca's birthday? ....
2. What types of fish does she like? ....
3. What types of shellfish does she like? ....
4. What types of fruit does she particularly like? ....
5. What city does she love? ....
6. What aspects of the city does she mention? ....
   ....
7. What does she like to wear (a) in winter and (b) in summer?
   (a) .... (b) ....
8. What types of films does she like?
   ....
9. What are her favourite possessions? ....
10. What does she like to do in her leisure time? ....
    ....

¡Vamos a escuchar 2!

27. Mensajes telefónicos (3)

You will hear three telephone messages.

🔊 54-56

1. What show is coming to town? ....
2. Where does José say there is a ticket office? ....
3. At what time does the show start? ....
4. What has he asked his girlfriend to do? ....

* * *

5. Where exactly did this girl find a mobile phone?
   ....
6. Describe the phone. ....
7. What telephone number does she ask the person to call? ....

* * *

8. When is this man's appointment with the doctor? ....
9. What does the receptionist ask the man to do? ....

¡Vamos a escuchar 2!

28. Una visita relámpago a Valencia

Marta and Paco plan a very busy day's sightseeing in Valencia!

🔊 57

1. What place does Marta suggest she and Paco could visit first?
   ....

2. What kind of museum is housed in the palace she mentions? ....

3. What size is the market? ....

4. What does Marta propose to buy there, and why?
   ....

5. In which area of the city are the Science Museum and the Aquarium?

   north ☐   south ☐   east ☐   west ☐

6. What number bus passes the Science Museum and Aquarium? ....

7. What did Marta's friend say about the restaurant in the Aquarium?
   ....

8. Where else would Marta have liked to have gone if they had had time?
   ....

¡Vamos a escuchar 2!

29. ¡Vaya fiasco de viaje!

Jaime phones his wife three times during a stressful business trip to Germany.

🔵 58–60

1. Jaime makes his first phone call from the departure lounge of the airport.
   True ☐   False ☐

2. What security measures are being implemented because a passenger has failed to turn up for the flight? ....
   ....

3. At what time does Jaime reckon he will arrive in Berlin? ....

* * *

4. What items did Jaime find in the suitcase he collected?
   ....

5. What is he concerned about? ....

* * *

6. At what time does Jaime reckon he will arrive home? ....

7. What does he say about the flight home?
   ....

8. What does he suggest to his wife? ....

33

¡Vamos a escuchar 2!

30. Rosa hace una entrevista

Rosa applies for a job as a sales assistant in a clothes shop.

🔘 61

1. What age is Rosa? ……………………………………………………………………
2. What is her address? …………………………………………………………………
3. What is her contact telephone number? ……………………………………………
4. What reason does she give for her fluency in English?
   ……………………………………………………………………………………………
5. Why is the shop owner interested in employing an assistant who speaks English?
   ……………………………………………………………………………………………
   ……………………………………………………………………………………………
6. What reasons does Rosa give for wanting to work in this clothes shop?
   ……………………………………………………………………………………………
   ……………………………………………………………………………………………

¡Vamos a escuchar 2!

7. Why has a former sales assistant left her job?

   ....

8. What qualities does the shop owner feel Rosa has? ....

   ....

9. On what basis does the shop owner offer Rosa a position in her shop?

   ....

   ....

10. On what day does the interview take place? ....

11. On what day and at what time will Rosa start work?

    ....

¡Vamos a escuchar 2!

31. ¿Por qué te llamas así?

Some young people are asked about their name.

🔊 62-64

1. How did Mari Carmen get her name? ....
   ....

2. She is the eldest in the family.   True ☐   False ☐

3. Why does she not like her name? ....
   ....

* * *

4. Why was this young man given the name 'Eusebio'?
   ....
   ....

5. Why does he not like his name?
   ....

* * *

6. On what date was Bárbara born? ....

7. Why was she called Bárbara?
   (i) ....
   (ii) ....

¡Vamos a escuchar 2!

32. Martín pide un favor a su madre

Martín asks his mother for a favour regarding some visitors to his town.

🔵 65

1. Who told Martín about these visitors, and when?
   ....
2. Why are the visitors coming to Seville?
   ....
3. When are they coming? ....
4. How long are they staying? ....
5. What favour does Martín ask of his mother?
   ....
6. Where is Martín's brother at the moment?
   ....
7. What suggestion does Martín's mother make?
   ....

¡Vamos a escuchar 2!

33. Anuncios (3)

You will hear three announcements.

🔴 66-68

1. What is the flight number of this plane? ....
2. Where is the plane coming from? ....
3. How long has it been delayed? ....
4. At what time will it arrive? ....
5. What has caused the delay? ....

* * *

6. What event has been cancelled? ....
7. Why has it been cancelled? ....
8. What kind of entertainment is being offered in its place by the television station? ....

* * *

9. Why has this train been delayed? ....
10. By how long has it been delayed? ....
11. At approximately what time is the train due to arrive? ....
12. What have the police told the public?
    ....

¡Vamos a escuchar 2!

34. En la oficina de turismo

A tourist has just arrived in town and has gone to the tourist office for information.

🔊 69

1. Supply the information that the tourist is given about each of the following places:

    (i) the church of San Martín ....

    (ii) the town hall ....

    (iii) the castle ....

    (iv) the botanic gardens ....

    ....

2. Why should the tourist not use a car?
   ....

3. What types of food do the restaurants in the Plaza Mayor serve?

    (i) .... (ii) ....

    (iii) ....

4. What is located near the main shopping complex? ....

5. What is the Calle Princesa famous for?

    (i) .... (ii) ....

6. What does the visitor ask the tourist officer to do? ....

¡Vamos a escuchar 2!

35. Un perro muy leal

You will hear the story of an extraordinary dog called Pícaro.

🔘 70

1. Where is this family from? ....
2. When did the family go on holiday? ....
3. They were staying:

    (a) in the country.   (b) in a hotel.   (c) on a camp-site.

    Put the correct letter in the box. ☐
4. What were the family doing when their dog Pícaro disappeared?

    ....
5. How long did they spend looking for him? ....
6. When did Pícaro appear at the door of their house? ....
7. How did he look? ....
8. What did he eat and drink? ....
9. How far do the family reckon he walked? ....
10. Where did a photo of Pícaro appear? ....
11. What has Pícaro been offered as a token of his loyalty, and by whom?

    ....

¡Vamos a escuchar 2!

36. Planes para el sábado

Rosario telephones her friend Merche to discuss plans for Saturday.

🔘 71

1. How far is Santillana del Mar from where the girls live? ....
2. Why should Rosario and Merche leave early in the day to visit Santillana del Mar? ....
3. Which bus does Rosario suggest that they take? ....
4. How long does the bus take to arrive in Santillana del Mar? ....
5. At what time does the last bus back leave Santillana del Mar? ....
6. How does Rosario suggest getting to her grandmother's house from Santillana del Mar? ....
7. What will Rosario bring her grandmother?
   ....
8. What does Merche suggest bringing Rosario's grandmother?
   ....
9. Where and when do the girls arrange to meet?
   ....

37. Philip Treacy: sombrerero extraordinario

You will hear about a world-famous Irish milliner, who makes exotic hats for women.

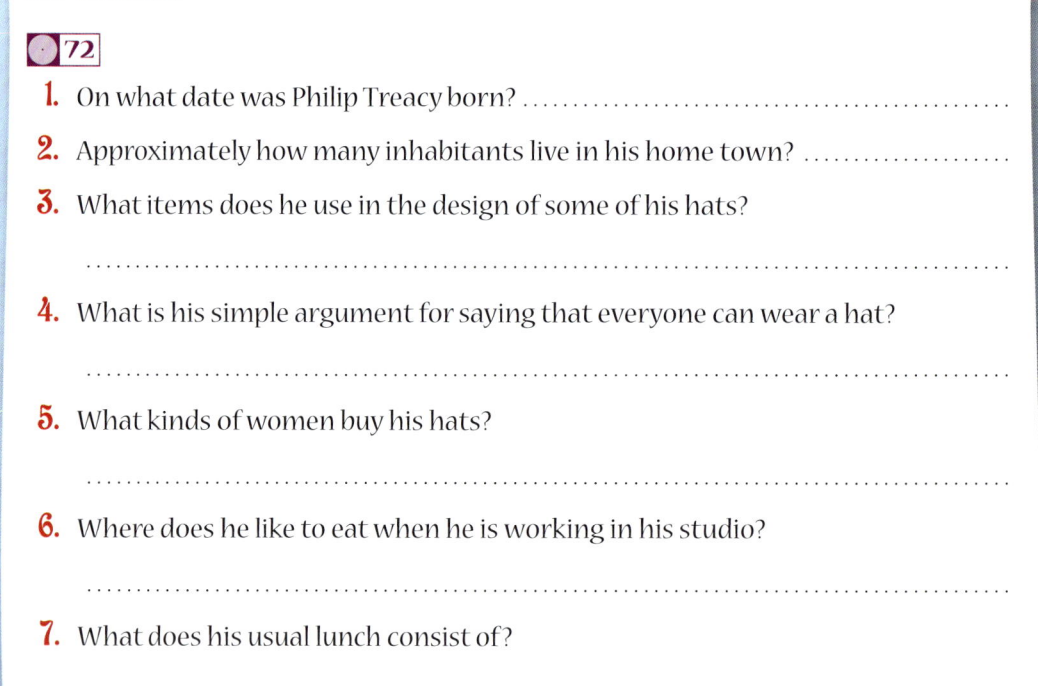

🔘 72

1. On what date was Philip Treacy born? ....

2. Approximately how many inhabitants live in his home town? ....

3. What items does he use in the design of some of his hats?
   ....

4. What is his simple argument for saying that everyone can wear a hat?
   ....

5. What kinds of women buy his hats?
   ....

6. Where does he like to eat when he is working in his studio?
   ....

7. What does his usual lunch consist of?
   ....

¡Vamos a escuchar 2!

38. En la oficina de objetos perdidos

Ana has lost her handbag and has gone to the lost property office to enquire about it.

🔘 73

1. What is Ana's handbag like? ....
2. What does it contain?
    (i) .... (ii) ....
    (iii) .... (iv) ....
3. How does she know that she had it in McDonald's?
    ....
4. Where did she go after she left McDonald's? ....
5. Where had she left her handbag? ....

¡Vamos a escuchar 2!

39. Dos sucesos desagradables

You will hear two telephone conversations. In each case something unfortunate has happened.

🔊 74–75

1. Who is telephoning la Sra. Benavente? ....
2. How and when did her daughter have an accident?
   ....
3. What injury has her daughter apparently sustained?
   ....
4. How far is the hospital from the scene of the accident? ....
5. What message does la Sra. Benavente give to her daughter?
   ....

* * *

6. What is this woman's address? ....
7. At what time did she leave her house? ....
8. Why did she go out? ....
9. What items does she say have been stolen?
   ....
10. When will a detective arrive? ....
11. What instruction is she given by the detective? ....

¡Vamos a escuchar 2!

40. Noticias (3)

You will hear three news items.

🔵 76–78

1. To what was this accident due? ....
2. How many people were injured? ....
3. How far from Madrid were the travellers at the time? ....
4. They were: (a) in cars.   (b) in a coach.   (c) in a train.
   Put the correct letter in the box. ☐
5. What event had they attended in Alcalá de Henares? ....

* * *

6. What country organised this film festival? ....
7. In which category did Miguel Estévez receive an award? ....
8. Why could Estévez not attend the festival?
   ....

* * *

9. Who organised this competition? ....
10. How many people have entered already? ....
11. From what countries have entries been submitted? ....
    ....
12. What must competitors send the organiser? ....
13. When is the closing date of the competition? ....

¡Vamos a escuchar 2!

41. Champiñones rellenos

You will hear a recipe for stuffed mushrooms.

🔘 79

1. Fill in the missing information in the grid.

QUANTITY	INGREDIENT
	mushrooms
	cloves of garlic
	chopped parsley
A little	

2. What exactly is the first instruction given?

   ....
   ....

3. The oven must be heated to .... degrees.

4. How long should the stuffed mushrooms be left in the oven? ....

¡Vamos a escuchar 2!

42. La casa donde vivo

Lola describes her house.

🔊 80

1. In what direction is San Lorenzo de El Escorial in relation to Madrid?
   ....

2. How far is San Lorenzo de El Escorial from Madrid? ....

3. According to Lola, why do few people live in houses in and around Madrid?
   ....

4. Describe the area in front of her house.
   ....

5. What information does she give regarding the patio at the back of her house?
   ....
   ....

¡Vamos a escuchar 2!

6. What rooms does she mention on the ground floor? ....
   ....
7. What does her father do for a living? ....
8. Who uses the spare bedroom? ....
9. Why does Lola like the area in which she lives? ....
   ....
   ....
10. How far above sea level is the place where she lives? ....
11. Why does she feel lonely at times?
    ....

¡Vamos a escuchar 2!

43. El tiempo (2)

You will hear a weather forecast.

🔊 81

Área de Madrid

1. Winds will be: light ☐   east. ☐
   from the
   strong ☐   west. ☐

2. What will the weather be like (a) in the morning and (b) for the rest of the day?

   (a) ....

   (b) ....

La Rioja

3. Describe weather conditions in La Rioja (a) early in the day and (b) later in the day.

   (a) ....

   (b) ....

Navarra

4. In the Pyrenees there will be: light ☐   showers. ☐
                                     heavy ☐   snow. ☐

¡Vamos a escuchar 2!

Baleares

5. Describe the weather conditions forecast for the Baleares.

....

Galicia

6. The weather will be less: windy ☐ foggy ☐

frosty ☐ sunny ☐ than before.

7. Describe weather conditions (a) early in the day and (b) later in the day.

(a) ....

(b) ....

¡Vamos a escuchar 2!

44. Cosas que me fastidian

Three people say what annoys them.

🔊 82-84

1. Speaker (a) hates ....
   because ....
   She also hates ....
   because ....

   * * *

2. Speaker (b) hates ....
   because ....
   He also hates ....
   because ....

   * * *

3. Speaker (c) hates..
   because ....
   She also hates ....
   because ....

¡Vamos a escuchar 2!

45. Mensajes de texto

You will hear some information regarding text messaging.

🔘 85

1. From what country is Matti Makkonen? ....
2. Give details of exactly where he was when he invented text messaging.

   ....

3. What letter is not usually used in Spanish text messaging? ....
4. What letter is typically used instead of 'll'? ....
5. What is said about question marks and exclamation marks?

   ....

6. How is *te quiero mucho* (I love you very much) typically expressed? ....
7. What do many teachers complain about?

   ....

8. What do other teachers argue is a positive aspect of text messaging?

   ....

¡Vamos a escuchar 2!

46. Cuando era niña

Manolito has to do a school project on what life was like in Spain in his grandparents' time.

🔵 86

1. How long does Manolito's grandmother say she would need in order to talk about life when she was young? ....

2. His grandmother starts by mentioning three ways in which life was different when she was young. What are they?

    (i) ....

    (ii) ....

    (iii) ....

3. What did a woman have to do if she wanted to work outside the home?
    ....
    ....

4. When did this situation change? ....

5. What examples does Manolito's grandmother give of certain things that were illegal then?
    ....
    ....

¡Vamos a escuchar 2!

6. What does she say about the type of government then and its effect?

....

....

7. What does she say about the situation now? ....

....

8. When she was young, how did (i) the Catholic church and (ii) the practice of religion differ from now?

(i) ....

(ii) ....

¡Vamos a escuchar 2!

47. Una excursión de fin de curso

A teacher makes an announcement about a school trip.

🔘 87

1. Give the (i) place, (ii) day, (iii) date and (iv) time the students must meet.

    (i) place .... (ii) day ....

    (iii) date .... (iv) time ....

2. What two monuments will they visit in Segovia?

    (i) .... (ii) ....

3. At what time will they eat? ....

4. What does the teacher suggest that the students might do in the afternoon?
    ....

5. That night the students will stay:

    (a) in a camp-site.   (b) in a hotel.

    (c) in a guesthouse.   (d) in a youth hostel.

    Put the correct letter in the box. ☐

¡Vamos a escuchar 2!

6. What accommodation is arranged in Salamanca? ....
7. What does the teacher say regarding (i) alcohol and (ii) smoking?
   (i) ....
   (ii) ....
8. What age are the students? ....
9. What did a student do last year without permission?
   ....
10. What was the result? ....

48. Planes para el verano

Mónica and Ricardo discuss their summer plans.

🔘 88

1. On what date will Mónica visit her aunt? ....
2. How long will she stay in Ireland? ....
3. In what circumstances did her aunt go to Ireland? ....
   ....
4. How many children does her aunt have? ....
5. What does Mónica plan to do during her trip? ....
   ....
   ....
6. For what two reasons has Ricardo decided to work in France?
   (i) ....
   (ii) ....
7. What will his job consist of? ....
8. What advantage does his job have? ....
9. Why does Mónica break off the conversation? ....

¡Vamos a escuchar 2!

49. Regalos de Navidad

Four people talk about the gifts they received last Christmas.

2–5

1. What did the parents of this girl secretly organise just before Christmas?
   ....

2. What did they buy their daughter? ....
   ....

3. Why is she delighted with her presents? ....
   ....
   ....

* * *

4. What 'gift' does this man say he and his wife received on Christmas Day?
   ....

* * *

5. Why is Christmas Day particularly special for this girl?
   ....

¡Vamos a escuchar 2!

6. What did she receive last Christmas from: (i) her parents? (ii) her brothers and sisters? (iii) her grandparents?

   (i) .... (ii) ....

   (iii) ....

* * *

7. What presents did this man give to his wife? ....
   ....

8. What presents did his wife give to him?
   ....
   ....

9. What did he receive from his brother? ....

10. What comment does he make regarding the present he received from his brother?
    ....

¡Vamos a escuchar 2!

50. En un restaurante

Paco and María José treat themselves to dinner in a restaurant.

🔊 6

1. What do Paco and María José order for their first course?

    María José ………………………………… Paco …………………………………

2. What kind of soup do they order?

    María José ………………………………… Paco …………………………………

3. What does María José first order for her main course? …………………………

4. Why does she change her mind? ………………………………………………

5. What does she order instead? …………………………………………………

6. What does Paco order for his main course? ……………………………………

7. What accompanies the main course? ……………………………………………

8. What beverages does Paco order?

    ……………………………………………………………………………………

¡Vamos a escuchar 2!

9. What flavours of ice-cream are available?

(i) .... (ii) ....

(iii) .... (iv) ....

(v) .... (vi) ....

10. What dessert does Paco order? ....

11. What aspect of the meal is María José not satisfied with?

....

¡Vamos a escuchar 2!

51. Vuelta a España

Irene has just returned to Spain from Ireland, and telephones her friend Begoña.

🔊 7

1. When did Irene return to Spain? ....
2. How far from Dublin was she staying? ....
3. Give details of the family she was staying with.
   ....
4. Apart from babysitting, what did Irene do to help during her stay in Ireland?
   (i) .... (ii) ....
   (iii) ....
5. How does Irene describe Irish people? ....
6. What is her opinion of Irish weather, and why?
   ....
7. In what way does Irene say the Irish and Spanish diet differs?
   ....
8. What establishments does she say close earlier in Ireland than in Spain?
   (i) .... (ii) ....
   (iii) ....
9. Irene thinks the telephone charges in Ireland are high.　True ☐　False ☐
10. Where, and at what time, do the girls arrange to meet?
    ....

¡Vamos a escuchar 2!

52. Accidentes de tráfico

You will hear some information regarding fatal traffic accidents.

🔊 8

1. What statistic is given regarding the number of fatal traffic accidents worldwide? ....
2. By how much is it estimated that this rate will increase over the next few years?
   ....
3. What statistic is given regarding the number of fatal traffic accidents in Spain?
   ....
4. In what position does Spain rank in Europe with respect to the rate of traffic fatalities? ....
5. Which European countries have a higher rate of fatal traffic accidents than Spain? ....
6. According to this report, what are the most common causes of traffic accidents?
   ....
   ....
   ....
   ....

¡Vamos a escuchar 2!

53. En el mercado

La Sra. Sotelo has gone to the local market to do some shopping.

9–11

1. Give details of the meat that la Sra. Sotelo buys. ....
   ....

* * *

2. What vegetables does she buy?
   ....

3. Apart from strawberries, what varieties of fruit does she wish to buy?
   ....

4. Why does she not buy strawberries? ....

* * *

5. What ingredients does the fishmonger's mother-in-law use when preparing paella? ....

6. Give exact details of what la Sra. Sotelo buys from the fishmonger.
   (i) .... (ii) ....
   (iii) .... (iv) ....

¡Vamos a escuchar 2!

54. Facebook

You will hear some information about a very popular website: Facebook.

🔊 12

1. When was this website set up by a Harvard university student? ....
2. What was his intention in setting it up? ....
   ....
3. How many new users join Facebook every week? ....
4. What percentage of its users use it on a daily basis? ....
5. What kinds of social groups use Facebook? ....
   ....
   ....
6. Approximately how many native Spanish speakers use the Internet on a regular basis? ....
7. How is the Facebook website financed? ....
8. What did a recent survey reveal, with respect to its popularity? ....
   ....

¡Vamos a escuchar 2!

55. Noticias (4)

You will hear three news items.

🔊 13–15

1. How many people died in this car bomb attack? ....
2. In what country did the attack occur? ....
3. What building was targeted? ....
4. How many terrorists were involved in the attack? ....
5. Give details of those who died. ....
   ....
6. What have the terrorists threatened to do?
   ....

* * *

7. How many attacks are estimated to have been carried out in Spain by skinheads this year? ....
8. Give details of those being victimised.
   ....
9. Who was attacked yesterday?
   ....

¡Vamos a escuchar 2!

10. Where did the attack occur? ....
11. Describe the attackers. ....

* * *

12. Where was this newborn baby found? ....
13. Give details of the finder, Juan Jiménez.
    ....
14. What alerted the finder to the baby's presence? ....
15. How are the police involved? ....
16. What statement has the finder made? ....
    ....

¡Vamos a escuchar 2!

56. El botellón

You will hear some information about the drinking habits of some young people in Spain.

🔘 16

1. What has the traditional attitude to alcoholic drink been in Spain?

   ....

2. Where and when do some young people congregate in Spain to drink alcohol?

   ....

3. Why is this habit called *'el botellón'*?

   ....
   ....

4. For what reasons do some young people take part in this social habit?

   ....
   ....

¡Vamos a escuchar 2!

5. What may be some of the consequences for those taking part?

....

....

6. What do some neighbours complain about? ....

....

7. What measures have some local governments taken to try to curb this social habit?

   (i) ....

   (ii) ....

   (iii) ....

¡Vamos a escuchar 2!

57. En el cámping

El Sr. Vilas has just arrived at a camp-site and is booking in.

🔵 17

1. For how long does this family intend to stay at the camp-site? ....
2. What does the attendant ask el Sr. Vilas to give her? ....
3. When will the family move their caravan?
   ....
4. Why will they move it? ....
5. What amenities does the camp-site offer?
   (i) .... (ii) ....
   (iii) .... (iv) ....
   (v) .... (vi) ....
6. When is there entertainment organised for children?
   ....
7. What exactly is organised for adults? ....
   ....

¡Vamos a escuchar 2!

8. What entertainment can children enjoy in the nearby town?

(i) ………………………………… (ii) …………………………………………

(iii) …………………………………

9. What is the first rule that the attendant mentions to el Sr. Vilas?

………………………………………………………………………………………

10. What other rules does the attendant mention?

………………………………………………………………………………………

………………………………………………………………………………………

¡Vamos a escuchar 2!

58. Una riña

Pepe telephones his girlfriend Begoña and a quarrel ensues.

🔊 18

1. What does Begoña plan to do this evening? ....
   ....
2. What does she plan to do with her friend tomorrow, and why?
   ....
3. What must she do on Saturday morning? ....
4. Where is she going on Saturday evening? ....
5. With whom is she going? ....
6. What does she accuse Pepe of? ....

¡Vamos a escuchar 2!

59. La dieta española

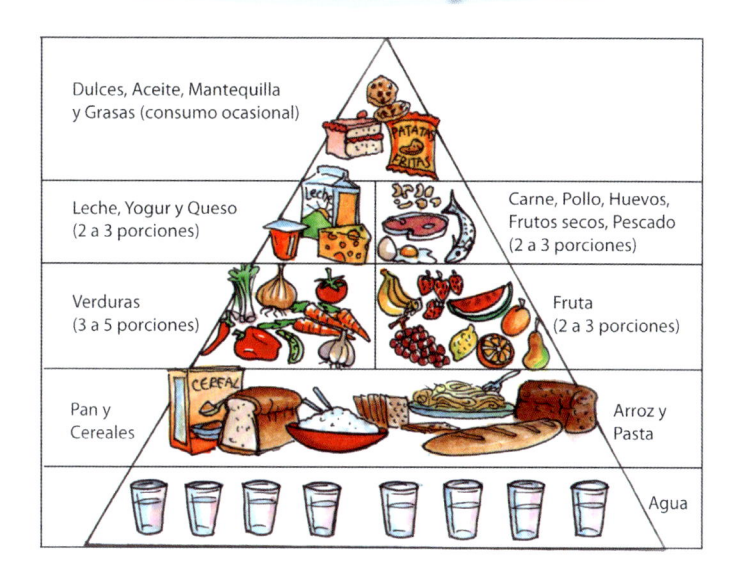

You will hear some information regarding changes in eating habits in Spain.

🔘 19

1. What traditional elements of the Mediterranean diet are still popular in Spain?

   ....

2. What nutritious foods have declined in popularity?

   ....

3. What information is given regarding the rise in obesity among Spanish children?

   ....

4. What reasons are given for the change in Spanish eating habits?

   (i) ....

   (ii) ....

   ....

   (iii) ....

   ....

¡Vamos a escuchar 2!

60. En el piso de al lado

Some people describe their next-door neighbour.

🔊 20–22

1. What age is this girl's next-door neighbour? ....
2. Describe this woman. ....
3. What is her profession? ....
4. Where does she go every weekend, and why?
   ....
5. Why is her job hampered nowadays?
   ....
   ....

* * *

6. What is the profession of this person's next-door neighbour?
   ....
7. What age is this man? ....
8. What does he look like? ....

¡Vamos a escuchar 2!

9. What advantages does his profession bring this person's family?
   ....
   ....

10. What disadvantage does it bring?
    ....

* * *

11. What country is this girl's neighbour from? ....
12. When did her neighbour leave her own country? ....
13. Why exactly did she leave it?
    ....

14. In what way does she say the quality of life in Spain is better for her children?
    ....

15. Why does this woman prefer the Spanish personality to that of her compatriots? ....
16. What does she think of her apartment, and why? ....
    ....

¡Vamos a escuchar 2!

61. Noticias (5)

You will hear three news items.

🔊 23–25

1. How many illegal immigrants were found by the police? ....
2. What were the immigrants trying to do? ....
3. What did the Red Cross do? ....

* * *

4. What age and nationality was the child who died? ....
5. How did the tragic accident happen? ....
6. When did the accident occur? ....
7. What did the parents think that the child was doing at the time of the accident?
   ....
8. How many children have died in this way in Spain this month? ....

* * *

9. How many people have been arrested by the police? ....
10. What country are these people from? ....
11. Where were counterfeit goods found? ....
12. Give details of the goods found.   (i) ....
    (ii) ....   (iii) ....
    (iv) ....   (v) ....

¡Vamos a escuchar 2!

62. Un cliente poco contento

A hotel manageress has to deal with a very dissatisfied customer.

🔘 26

1. When did this visitor arrive at the hotel? ....
2. What complaints does he make regarding room service?
    (i) .... (ii) ....
3. What does the manageress say by way of explanation?
    ....
4. What does he say was wrong with the breakfast?
    (i) .... (ii) ....
5. What excuse does the manageress give?
    ....
    ....
6. Where did the visitor go that morning? ....
7. What did he discover on his return?
    ....

¡Vamos a escuchar 2!

8. What annoyed him the previous night? ....
9. What defence does the manageress offer?
   ....
10. How does she describe the hotel? ....
11. What suggestion does she make to the visitor?
    ....

¡Vamos a escuchar 2!

63. Medina Azahara

You will hear information about one of the most magnificent palace-cities of its time in the world.

🔊 27

1. How far from Córdoba was Medina Azahara situated? ....
2. In what year was Medina Azahara founded? ....
3. How many people were involved in its construction? ....
4. How many years did it take to complete? ....
5. What precious stones decorated the marble walls? ....
6. How many doors led to the central chamber? ....
7. What size were the gardens? ....
8. What did the gardens contain?
   ....
9. In what year was Medina Azahara sacked by a North African tribe? ....
10. When was Medina Azahara rediscovered? ....
11. How many tourists now visit Medina Azahara annually? ....

¡Vamos a escuchar 2!

64. Maite toma parte en un concurso de radio

Maite takes part in a radio quiz in the hope of winning a prize.

◉ 28

A radio presenter asks Maite eight questions. What are they, and what correct answer does she give to each?

1. Q. ....
   A. ....
2. Q. ....
   A. ....
3. Q. ....
   A. ....
4. Q. ....
   A. ....
5. Q. ....
   A. ....

¡Vamos a escuchar 2!

6. Q. ....
A. ....

7. Q. ....
A. ....

8. Q. ....
A. ....

¡Vamos a escuchar 2!

65. ¿De verdad? ¡Sí!

You will hear some incredible information about real events that happened.

🔊 29–31

1. What did this Indonesian multimillionaire wish to promote?
   ....

2. Where had people gathered near Jakarta to collect the money that he distributed? ....

3. The money that he distributed was the equivalent of €6000.
   True ☐   False ☐

* * *

4. In what country did this robber hypnotise a cashier? ....

5. What was the last thing the girl remembers him saying?
   ....

6. Approximately how much did the man steal? ....

7. What was his approximate age? ....

8. Where do the police believe him to be from?
   .... or ....

* * *

¡Vamos a escuchar 2!

9. What age was this Japanese man? ....
10. What did he notice? ....
11. What did the security camera in his house reveal was happening, and when?
    ....
12. What else did the man discover?
    ....

¡Vamos a escuchar 2!

66. El Sr. Lázaro va de compras

El Sr. Lázaro goes shopping to buy some clothes.

🔘 32

1. What colour of suit is this man looking for? ....
2. Specify the material he wants. ....
3. What size of suit does he wear? ....
4. What price is the suit he is shown? ....
5. What exactly does he find wrong with the suit he is shown?
   ....
6. What kind of tie is he looking for?
   (a) material .... (b) colour ....
7. What does he find wrong with the range in this shop?
   ....
8. What does the shop assistant say about the style of tie that the customer is looking for?
   ....

¡Vamos a escuchar 2!

67. El día que más recuerdo

Some people remember a special event in their lives.

🔊 33–35

1. What event did this girl attend? ....
2. Where did the event take place? ....
3. What item was thrown in the air during the event? ....
4. How did this girl feel when she caught it? ....
5. How do her friends feel about it? ....
6. Where exactly is the item now? ....
7. What do her friends want to do when they visit her?
   ....

* * *

8. What saint's feast day will this man always remember? ....
9. Why was the day special for this man?
   ....
10. Describe the item that he bought.
    ....
11. Where did he go that night and with whom?
    ....

85

¡Vamos a escuchar 2!

12. What were these people given, and by whom?

....

* * *

13. Why was the arrival of this baby an extra special event for this girl's family?

....

14. What did her grandparents do? ....

15. What did the neighbours buy the baby? ....

16. What did her father buy the baby? ....

17. What reason did he give for this purchase? ....

....

¡Vamos a escuchar 2!

68. El Tibidabo

You will hear some information about a well-known mountain in Cataluña.

🔘 36

1. How high is the Tibidabo? ....
2. What can be seen from the top? ....
3. Why did Saint John Bosco climb the Tibidabo?

   ....

4. In what year did Queen María Cristina climb it? ....
5. Why was she in the area at the time? ....
6. What two means of transport made the Tibidabo accessible to the general public?

   (i) .... (ii) ....

7. Who financed this transport? ....
8. Why do people visit the Tibidabo? ....

   ....

¡Vamos a escuchar 2!

69. Una pequeña visita a Francia

Paula is about to visit relatives in France, and her mother is checking that she has everything ready.

🔵 37

1. What does Paula have in her bag?

   (i) .... (ii) ....

   (iii) ....

2. What presents does she have for her relatives?

   (a) aunt ....

   (b) uncle ....

   (c) cousins ....

3. What does her mother tell her to do when she arrives?

   ....

4. How does her mother suggest that Paula can help while she is there?

   ....

¡Vamos a escuchar 2!

5. What exactly does her mother say to her regarding food?
　　..

6. What should Paula tell her uncle and aunt if she gets sick?
　　..

7. At what time is her plane leaving? ....

8. How long is she staying in France? ....

¡Vamos a escuchar 2!

70. El tiempo (3)

You will hear a weather forecast.

🔊 38

1. On what date and at what time will autumn officially begin?

   ....

2. In the north of Spain there will be a: rise ☐   in temperature
                                              fall ☐

   with a(n)   increase ☐   in cloud with   showers. ☐
               decrease ☐   drizzle. ☐

3. On what days will the weather start to become more unsettled?

   ....

4. When will this situation spread to the rest of Spain?

   ....

5. Describe the weather forecast for the northern part of Spain on Sunday.

   ....

¡Vamos a escuchar 2!

71. El sitio que más me gusta

You will hear three people talking about their favourite place.

🔊 39–41

1. What place does this young woman like?
   ....
2. How does she describe the atmosphere there? ....
3. What does she think is unusual about the place?
   ....

* * *

4. What place does this person like best?
   ....
5. What can he do there?
   ....
   ....

* * *

6. What is this girl's favourite place? ....
7. Why does she dislike being at home? ....
   ....

¡Vamos a escuchar 2!

72. Exámenes

You will hear ten tips to help students to prepare for an examination.

◯ 42

1. What is the first advice that is given?

   ....

   ....

2. What advice is given regarding one's study environment?

   ....

3. What advice is given regarding study breaks?

   ....

4. When is it advisable not to study? ....

5. When preparing for an examination, what should one try to do every day?

   ....

6. What type of food should be avoided? ....

7. What is said regarding tea and coffee? ....

8. What affects one's memory and concentration? ....

9. What should one do after finishing one's studies every night? ....

   ....

¡Vamos a escuchar 2!

10. What advice is given regarding sleep?

....

11. What is said with regard to friends and family? ....

....

12. What final advice is given with respect to examinations?

....

¡Vamos a escuchar 2!

73. Noticias (6)

You will hear three news items.

🔊 43–45

1. What did this earthquake register on the Richter scale? ....
2. How long did the earthquake last? ....
3. Give details of the injured and dead. ....
4. What did thousands of people have to do, and why?
   ....
5. What services have been interrupted? ....
6. What has the national meteorological service stated?
   ....

* * *

7. What kind of plane was involved in this crash? ....
8. In what city did the crash occur? ....
9. Give details of those who were killed. ....
10. At what time did the accident occur? ....
11. What age was the pilot? ....
12. How did the pilot manage to escape? ....
13. What was the nature of his injuries? ....

¡Vamos a escuchar 2!

14. Why has a government commission been set up?

....

* * *

15. What country has won the Eurovision Song Contest? ....
16. How many votes did it receive? ....
17. What country came second? ....
18. How many votes did the country in second position receive? ....
19. What age was the singer who represented Spain? ....
20. In what position did Spain finish? ....
21. In what year did Spain first win the Eurovision Song Contest? ....
22. Why did the singer, Joan Manuel Serrat, pull out of the competition that year?

....

¡Vamos a escuchar 2!

74. ¿Cómo pasas las Navidades?

Some people describe how they spend Christmas.

🔊 46–49

1. When does this person's family feel that Christmas has started?
   ....
2. Who comes to visit this family on Christmas Eve? ....
3. What does the first course always consist of? ....
4. What does the main course consist of? .... or ....
5. Why does the speaker not like *turrón*? ....
6. Where does the family go after dinner? ....

* * *

7. Why does this person's family not spend a lot on presents?
   ....
8. Give details of what this person's brothers do on the night of the 5th of January.
   ....
   ....

* * *

¡Vamos a escuchar 2!

9. What is the aim of the organisation that this girl belongs to?
   ....
10. Whom do they visit at Christmas? ....
    ....
11. What do they do during their visit?
    ....
12. Whom do the older members of the organisation also visit?
    ....
13. What kinds of presents do they bring?
    ....

* * *

14. What relatives arrive to celebrate Christmas with this family?
    ....
15. What two things do the children organise?
    (i) .... (ii) ....
16. What food is eaten? ....
17. What drink is served? ....

¡Vamos a escuchar 2!

75. Anuncios (4)

You will hear three announcements.

🔊 50–52

1. What is the consequence of the snowfall in north-west Spain?

   ....

2. What are drivers in northern Spain advised to do, and why?

   ....

3. How long is this situation likely to continue?

   ....

* * *

4. What is the flight number of this plane? ....

5. Where is it going? ....

6. What exactly are passengers told to do? ....

   ....

* * *

7. Where is this announcement being made? ....

8. What has happened? ....

9. What two things are people advised to do?

   (i) .... (ii) ....

10. What two things are people advised **not** to do?

    (i) .... (ii) ....

¡Vamos a escuchar 2!

76. Un día catastrófico

Elena tells her friend Merche about her awful day, but ends up feeling much better!

🔘 53

1. Why did Elena go to an Italian boutique? ....
2. Supply details of the dress she bought.

    Colour ....   Pattern ....

    Size ....   Price ....

3. Where did she leave the dress by mistake?

    ....

4. What comment does she make regarding the person who took her dress?

    ....

5. How much was she fined for parking her car in the wrong place? ....
6. Where had she parked her car? ....
7. Describe the girl who was with Elena's boyfriend.

    ....

8. What had Paco told Elena the previous day?

    ....

¡Vamos a escuchar 2!

77. Unas costumbres españolas

You will hear some people talking about certain Spanish customs. Some are rather curious!

🔊 54–56

1. This person is talking about:

   (a) New Year's Eve.   (b) New Year's Day.

   (c) Christmas Eve.   (d) Midsummer Night.

   Put the correct letter in the box. ☐

2. Where do people gather? ....

3. What exactly do they do?

   ....

4. What do a lot of young people wear? ....

5. The garment(s) must be:

   (a) a present.   (b) old.   (c) borrowed.   (d) new.

   Put the correct letter in the box. ☐

6. Why might it be difficult to get items of clothing like this?

   ....

* * *

¡Vamos a escuchar 2!

7. In what region of Spain does this young man live? ....
8. A bride carries a bouquet of:

   (a) lilies.   (b) orange blossom.   (c) rosebuds.   (d) carnations.

   Put the correct letter in the box. ☐
9. What is believed to bring bad luck? ....
10. What happens when the bride and groom leave the church?

    ....
11. What do the groom's friends do at the end of the reception, and why?

    ....

    ....

* * *

12. What journey does a hearse take in this town?

    ....
13. What two things happen when the hearse passes? ....

    ....
14. What customs used to prevail in the deceased's own house? ....

    ....

¡Vamos a escuchar 2!

78. El tiempo (4)

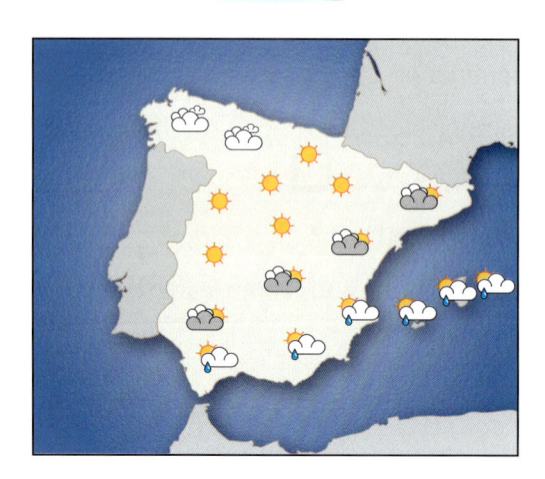

You will hear a weather forecast.

🕐 57

Cataluña

1. It will be: misty ☐   morning. ☐
   　　　　　　foggy ☐   in the   afternoon. ☐
   　　　　　　cloudy ☐   evening. ☐

2. Rain will be: light ☐   heavy. ☐

Madrid

3. Describe weather conditions in the Sierra. ....
4. It will be mainly cloudy for most of the day.   True ☐   False ☐

Galicia

5. What will conditions in mountainous areas be like?

   ....

¡Vamos a escuchar 2!

6. From what direction will the wind blow? ……………………………………

7. Temperatures in central Spain will be …………… maximum and …………… minimum.

8. Temperatures in mountainous areas will be …………… maximum and …………… minimum.

¡Vamos a escuchar 2!

79. La persona que más admiro

Marisol talks about the person she most admires.

🔘 58

1. What is Javier's attitude to life? ....
2. In what way does he help his classmates?
   ....
3. What position does he hold in his school?
   ....
4. What are his other interests?
   ....
5. Who organised the competition he has just won?
   ....
6. What topic did the competitors have to write about?
   ....
7. What was the essence of Javier's winning entry?
   ....
   ....

¡Vamos a escuchar 2!

8. When should Javier have collected his prize? ....

9. What prevented him from doing so?

....

10. How will he get his prize? ....

11. What was his reaction to not being able to collect his prize in person?

....

....

¡Vamos a escuchar 2!

80. Algunas fiestas locales de España

You will hear about three Spanish festivals.

🔊 59-61

1. Between what dates are the *Fallas* celebrated? ....
2. What happens to the satirical cardboard figures that are seen on the streets?
   ....
3. Give details of the offering of flowers to the Virgin Mary.
   ....
   ....
4. In what other ways are the *Fallas* celebrated? ....
   ....

* * *

5. In what month is the *Festival de los Patios* in Córdoba celebrated? ....
6. What does the local council do?
   ....

* * *

7. How far is Buñol from Valencia? ....
8. In approximately what year is the *Tomatina* festival believed to have begun?
   ....

¡Vamos a escuchar 2!

9. On what day of the year is it celebrated? ....
10. At what time do the celebrations begin? ....
11. Up to how many kilos of tomatoes are thrown? ....
12. Up to how many people throw tomatoes at each other? ....
13. What do people do when they finish throwing tomatoes?
    ....

¡Vamos a escuchar 2!

81. Unas gemelas extraordinarias

You will hear the remarkable true story of identical twins Dorothy and Bridget.

🔴 62

1. What is John Stroud's profession? ....

2. What is his particular area of work? ....
   ....

3. Why is his area of work uncommon nowadays? ....
   ....

4. What is Dr Bouchard's profession? ....

5. What does his research involve?
   ....
   ....

6. According to the text, Dorothy and Bridget:

   (a) had been searching for each other for 34 years.

   (b) had been in contact for 34 years without meeting.

   (c) were reunited after 34 years.

   Put the correct letter in the box. ☐

108

¡Vamos a escuchar 2!

7. Give details of the jewellery they were wearing when they met.
   ....

8. What similarities were there regarding each woman's wedding?
   ....

9. What coincidence existed regarding their children?
   ....

10. What coincidence existed regarding each family's pet?
    ....

11. What coincidence existed regarding a leisure activity they enjoyed?
    ....

¡Vamos a escuchar 2!

82. En la consulta

La Sra. Castaño visits the doctor.

🔊 63

1. What symptoms does the woman describe?
   ....

2. What does the doctor check first? ....

3. When does the patient forget to eat?
   ....

4. How many children does she have? ....

5. Between what ages are they? ....

6. Where is her husband at the moment? ....

7. The doctor tells his patient that she:

   (a) is suffering from exhaustion. (b) is dieting too much.

   (c) has an ulcer. (d) is not sleeping enough.

   Put the correct letter in the box. ☐

8. What foods does the doctor recommend?
   ....

¡Vamos a escuchar 2!

9. In what ways does he suggest her children can help her?
   (i) .... (ii) ....
   (iii) .... (iv) ....

10. What exercise is she advised to take?
    ....

11. How many cigarettes does she smoke daily? ....

12. What two reasons does her doctor give her for giving up smoking?
    (i) ....
    (ii) ....

13. When must the woman visit the doctor again?
    ....

¡Vamos a escuchar 2!

83. Noticias (7)

You will hear three news items.

🔵 64-66

1. What kind of plane was involved in this accident? ....
2. At what time did the accident happen? ....
3. How many people were injured? ....
4. From what country was the plane returning? ....
5. What was the cause of the accident? ....
   ....

* * *

6. From what Spanish city was Ramón Pascual Díaz? ....
7. How did he die? ....
8. What age was he when he died? ....
9. Give details of his widow. ....
10. Give details of his children. ....

* * *

¡Vamos a escuchar 2!

11. This man is:

(a) a tobacco smuggler. (b) a drug dealer.
(c) an art forger. (d) car dealer.

Put the correct letter in the box. ☐

12. What items is he accused of attempting to bring into Spain?

....

13. Where were the items hidden? ....

14. He is accused of three other crimes. What are they?

(i) .... (ii) ....

(iii) ....

113

¡Vamos a escuchar 2!

84. ¡Que aproveche!

Three people talk about their job which involves food or drink.

🔊 67–69

1. In what part of Spain does this man have his vineyards? ....

2. To what four factors does he owe the good quality of his sherry?

   (i) .... (ii) ....

   (iii) .... (iv) ....

3. Some people like to drink his sherry accompanied by:

   (a) prawns.   (b) olives.   (c) peanuts.   (d) raisins.

   Put the correct letter in the box. ☐

* * *

4. What products does this nun's community make?

   ....

5. What did the nuns of her community do in the past with these products?

   ....

6. What is the main ingredient used? ....

7. What other ingredients are used?

   ....

¡Vamos a escuchar 2!

8. How does her community advertise its products?
   ....

9. How do they know a customer has arrived?
   ....

* * *

10. Where does this man cook paella? ....

11. According to this man, what two factors give paella its distinctive flavour?
    (i) .... (ii) ....

12. What should not be done during cooking? ....

13. What does he consider the tastiest part of the paella?
    ....

¡Vamos a escuchar 2!

85. ¿La correspondencia más breve del mundo?

You will hear about the shortest correspondence in the world!

🔊 70

1. In what year did this correspondence take place? ……………………………………
2. To whom did Victor Hugo write? ……………………………………………
3. What did he wish to know?
   ………………………………………………………………………………………
4. What was the content of the postcard he sent? ……………………………………
5. What was the content of the reply? ……………………………………………
6. What message did he understand from the reply?
   ………………………………………………………………………………………

¡Vamos a escuchar 2!

86. Natalia se encuentra depre

Natalia feels a bit depressed and her friend Milagros makes some helpful suggestions.

🔊 71

1. In what ways does Natalia complain of being 'out of sorts'?
   ....
   ....

2. Where was Milagros when she read an article on depression?
   ....

3. According to the article, when are certain people most likely to get depressed?
   ....

4. How do some doctors treat their patients who are suffering from depression?
   ....

5. According to the article, what beverage, besides Coca Cola, should be limited?
   ....

6. What types of food should (a) be eaten and (b) not be eaten?
   (a) ....
   (b) ....

¡Vamos a escuchar 2!

7. What does Natalia think about the inclusion of sugar in her diet?
....

8. According to the article, what two things are 'taboo'?
....

9. How should someone start the day? ....

10. Why is walking in a park recommended?
....

11. Why does Natalia object to the idea of walking?
....

12. What is Natalia's view of the suggestions made in the article?
....

¡Vamos a escuchar 2!

87. Pepe y Concha hacen una lluvia de ideas sobre el medio ambiente

Pepe and Concha prepare some ideas for a class discussion on the environment.

🔘 72

1. When will the class discussion on the environment take place?
   ....

2. What four aspects of environmental damage does Concha first mention?
   (i) .... (ii) ....
   (iii) .... (iv) ....

3. Why does Pepe reject Concha's initial suggestions?
   ....

4. Besides plastic, what materials does Pepe suggest could be used less, reused or recyled? ....
   ....

5. In what way does Concha suggest the use of plastic could be reduced?
   ....
   ....

¡Vamos a escuchar 2!

6. What suggestion does Pepe make with respect to using one's car?
   ....

7. What measures does Concha say people at home can take to minimise the use of water?
   ....
   ....

8. In what other ways do Pepe and Concha suggest people can limit the use of energy at home?
   ....
   ....

9. Why does Pepe suggest going to the Puerta del Sol?
   ....

¡Vamos a escuchar 2!

88. Adolfo: ex drogadicto

Adolfo talks about the time when he was a drug addict.

🔊 73

1. Who invited Adolfo to speak to this group? ....
2. How long was Adolfo a drug addict? ....
3. What does he do now?

   ....

4. What was the first kind of drug he began taking? ....
5. Why did he start taking drugs?

   ....

6. According to Adolfo, why do some young people start taking drugs?

   (i) .... (ii) ....

   (iii) ....

7. By the end of the first year, how were drugs affecting his life? ....

   ....

8. How had his personality changed by the end of the second year?

   ....

¡Vamos a escuchar 2!

9. What did his father do? ....
10. What did Adolfo do to finance his addiction?
    ....
11. What news did he receive one day? ....
    ....
12. What realisation did he come to?
    ....
13. In what ways has his life changed since giving up drugs?
    ....
    ....
14. What does he tell the group (a) to do and (b) not to do?
    (a) .... (b) ....

¡Vamos a escuchar 2!

89. Mousse de verano

You will hear a recipe for a delicious dessert.

🔘 74

1. Give the exact ingredients used in this dessert.

    (i) ……………………………………   (ii) ……………………………………

    (iii) ……………………………………   (iv) ……………………………………

    (v) ……………………………………

2. What five instructions are given, regarding the preparation of the fruit?

    (i) ……………………………………   (ii) ……………………………………

    (iii) ……………………………………   (iv) ……………………………………

    (v) ……………………………………

3. How long should the dessert be left to chill? ……………………………………

4. How should the mousse be decorated?

    ………………………………………………………………………………………

¡Vamos a escuchar 2!

90. La mujer en la España actual

Four people give their view on the position of women in Spain today.

 75–78

1. In what ways is this woman not satisfied with the working conditions of the housewife in Spain?

    (i) ....

    (ii) ....

2. What is the attitude of her husband's colleagues and clients on meeting her?

    ....

* * *

3. In what year were women and men in Spain given equal constitutional rights?

    ....

4. In what four ways does this person say things have improved for women in Spain?

    (i) ....

    (ii) ....

    (iii) ....

    (iv) ....

¡Vamos a escuchar 2!

5. In the past a man might have been teased by friends if seen:

(i) ....

(ii) ....

(iii) ....

* * *

6. What occupations does this man say would rarely be held by women?

(i) .... (ii) ....

(iii) .... (iv) ....

7. What occupations would be held by women?

(i) .... (ii) ....

(iii) .... (iv) ....

8. This man's wife:

(a) makes handbags.   (b) works in the Stock Exchange.

(c) sells handbags.   (d) is a cashier.

Put the correct letter in the box. ☐

9. What is this man's view of the flirtatious remarks made by male colleagues to female colleagues?

....

* * *

10. According to this person, how have women in Spain changed since the Franco era?

(i) .... (ii) ....

(iii) ....

¡Vamos a escuchar 2!

11. Why does she think that men are reluctant to deal with women in the workforce?

Either because (a) ....

or because (b) ....

12. In what ways does this person believe inequality still exists in certain homes?

....

....

¡Vamos a escuchar 2!

91. El 11-M

You will hear some information regarding bombings which took place in crowed trains in and around Madrid, an event referred to as 'El 11-M'.

🔘 79

1. When exactly did this tragic event happen? ....
2. What event was scheduled to take place three days later?

   ....
3. Between what times did the explosions occur? .... and ....
4. How many people lost their lives in this tragedy? ....
5. How many people were injured? ....
6. When did protest marches take place? ....
7. How many people took to the streets of Madrid? ....
8. What dignitaries were among those who took part in the protest march in Madrid? ....

   ....

   ....

¡Vamos a escuchar 2!

9. The monument, erected outside Atocha station in memory of the victims, is:

(a) square.   (b) round.   (c) cylindrical.

Put the correct letter in the box. ☐

10. How high is the monument? ....

11. The monument is made of: (a) glass.   (b) metal.   (c) stone.

Put the correct letter in the box. ☐

12. What can visitors see when they access the monument from inside Atocha station?

(i) ....

(ii) ....

¡Vamos a escuchar 2!

92. Problemas actuales en España

Some people give their view on current problems in Spain.

🔘 80-82

1. How does this girl define a marginalised person? ....
   ....

2. What groups of people does she consider to be marginalised in Spain?
   (i) .... (ii) ....
   (iii) ....

3. According to this girl, how should society change? ....
   ....

* * *

4. What kinds of people are affected by unemployment in Spain, according to this boy? ....
   ....

5. Where did this boy's father work?
   ....

6. In what circumstances did he lose his job?
   ....

¡Vamos a escuchar 2!

7. How has unemployment affected (a) this man, (b) his wife and (c) his children?

(a) ....

(b) ....

(c) ....

* * *

8. Why have moral values declined in Spain, in this girl's opinion?

....

9. What does she see as evidence of this decline in moral standards?

....

....

....

¡Vamos a escuchar 2!

93. Las cuevas de Altamira

You will hear some information about the caves of Altamira.

🔘 83

1. In what area of Spain are the caves of Altamira situated? ....
2. In what year were they discovered? ....
3. How long are the caves? ....
4. Name two animals represented in the paintings.
   (i) .... (ii) ....
5. How are some figures represented?
   ....
6. What might these figures have been taking part in?
   ....
7. Name two colours used in the paintings. ....
8. Why were experts initially sceptical of the authenticity of the paintings?
   ....
9. What event made experts acknowledge their authenticity?
   ....